Guidelines

Three weeks of undated Bible reading

Text copyright © BRF 2003

Published by
The Bible Reading Fellowship
First Floor, Elsfield Hall
15–17 Elsfield Way, Oxford OX2 8FG
ISBN 1 84101 355 2

First published 2003
10 9 8 7 6 5 4 3 2 1
All rights reserved

Acknowledgments
Unless otherwise stated, scripture quotations are taken from The New Revised Standard Version of the Bible, Anglicized Edition, copyright © 1989, 1995 by the Division of Christian Education of the National Council of the Churches of Christ in the USA, and are used by permission. All rights reserved.

Scripture quotations taken from the *Holy Bible, New International Version*, copyright © 1973, 1978, 1984 by International Bible Society, are used by permission of Hodder & Stoughton Limited. All rights reserved. 'NIV' is a registered trademark of International Bible Society. UK trademark number 1448790.

Extracts from the Authorized Version of the Bible (The King James Bible), the rights in which are vested in the Crown, are reproduced by permission of the Crown's patentee, Cambridge University Press.

A catalogue record for this book is available from the British Library

Printed and bound in Malta

CONTENTS

Introduction 4

Guidelines contributors 5

The ministry of Jesus 6

The Sabbath 20

Also published by BRF 27

How to order BRF notes 28

INTRODUCTION TO GUIDELINES

The focus of our work here at BRF is helping people with Bible reading and prayer, as well as in understanding what it means to belong to the Christian Church. In reading the Bible, we learn more of how our faith fits together, and this can nurture our prayer life, both as individuals and as worshipping communities. Reading with the help of insightful comment from others can help us get more out of the Bible, challenge our assumptions, and bring us fresh insights into familiar passages.

This sampler offers three weeks of readings from our in-depth *Guidelines* notes, which represent a thought-provoking breadth of Christian tradition. *Guidelines* has two editors: Katharine Dell (Old Testament) is Senior Lecturer in the Faculty of Divinity at Cambridge University and Director of Studies in Theology at St Catherine's College; and John Parr (New Testament) is a mental health advocate and a theological educator. When reading *Guidelines* you will need a copy of the Bible to hand, as the passage is not included. The readings selected here are by Kenneth Bailey (The ministry of Jesus) and Jo Bailey Wells (The Sabbath).

I hope that you will enjoy using the sample readings, and that they will inspire you to deepen your commitment to regular Bible study and prayer.

Naomi Starkey

Managing Editor, Bible reading notes

GUIDELINES CONTRIBUTORS

Among recent contributors to *Guidelines* are:

Alec Gilmore, Baptist minister, former editor of Lutterworth Press and Director of the charity *Feed the Minds*. He is an adult education lecturer on biblical themes in Sussex University and author of *A Dictionary of the English Bible and its Origins* (Sheffield Academic Press).

Elizabeth Moore, an adult educator, presently working among members of the Anglican Church in Suffolk. Before that she was Lecturer in Old Testament and Vice-Principal of Lincoln Theological College.

Gordon McConville, Professor in Old Testament Studies in the University of Gloucestershire. He has written books on Deuteronomy and the historical books of the Old Testament.

Jo Bailey Wells, a Tutor at Ridley Hall, Cambridge, and Lecturer in Old Testament for the Cambridge Theological Federation. She was previously Dean of Clare College and is married with a young child.

Andrew Gregory, Chaplain and Oakeshott Junior Research Fellow at Lincoln College, Oxford, and a member of the Oxford Theology Faculty. He teaches New Testament and has written articles for the *Church of England Newspaper*.

Hugh Williamson, Regius Professor of Hebrew at the University of Oxford.

Frances Briscoe, a retired Anglican priest and former teacher of Religious Education, who has held parochial, cathedral and diocesan posts and has been involved in the training of clergy, ordinands and readers.

Gordon Mursell, Dean of Birmingham Cathedral. He taught spirituality at a theological college for five years and has written a number of books including *Out of the Deep: Prayer as Protest* (DLT, 1989) and *English Spirituality* (2 volumes, SPCK 2001).

Henry Wansbrough, OSB, the Master of St Benet's Hall, Oxford, a writer, broadcaster and General Editor of *The New Jerusalem Bible*. He is also a General Editor of BRF's *People's Bible Commentary* series and the author of *Luke* in that series.

THE MINISTRY OF JESUS: INAUGURATION AND DRAMA

For two weeks we will be reflecting on the inauguration of the public ministry of Jesus as it is recorded in Luke 4:16–31. This is a rich and densely packed passage worthy of an attempt to unlock at least a few of its secrets. One of the keys to those secrets is a recently published fragment of a scroll found among the famous Dead Sea Scrolls. This tiny scrap of pre-Christian papyrus describes the coming Messiah as one who will 'preach good news to the poor' and provide 'release for the captives'. He will also 'open the eyes of the blind' and 'raise up the downtrodden'. A second fragment from the same cave mentions that the 'Holy Spirit rests on his Messiah'. The text from Isaiah that Jesus selects to read in the synagogue in Nazareth is clearly in tune with the expectations of the Jewish visionaries of his day. But there is a problem.

At first, the listening congregation appears to like what Jesus reads and what he says about the text. Yet within a few minutes they are trying to stone him. Why? What turns an apparently pleased congregation into a mob of killers? This week will be devoted to searching for answers to this question.

Jesus in the synagogue

1 The Spirit of the Lord is upon me

Luke 4:16–19 and Isaiah 61:1–2

In this scene Jesus inaugurates his public ministry. For more than a decade Jesus was, in all likelihood, a member of the *khabureem* (the friends), a Jewish lay study fellowship spread across the villages of the land. At the age of 30, Jesus presents himself to John for baptism during which the Spirit descends upon him (3:22) and a voice from heaven confirms him as the approved Son of God.

After this confirmation and empowerment, Jesus returns to Galilee. He appears in his home village and attends sabbath worship in the local synagogue. It was customary for worship leaders to invite a worthy person in the congregation to read and comment on the day's scriptures. Jesus is so invited and selects a well-known text. As we will see, it contains the agenda upon which the village was most likely founded. The reader was allowed, particularly in the Prophets, to do a bit of pious editing as he read. Jesus uses this privilege astutely. Thus that which Luke records is not precisely what Isaiah wrote but may well reflect what Jesus actually read. It is our responsibility to look with great care at what Jesus selected and how he edited the verses chosen.

Jesus begins with the bold words, 'The Spirit of the Lord is upon me!' Either this amazing claim is right and Jesus is to be followed, or it is arrogant and presumptuous and this young rabbi is a proud and dangerous man. There is no ground between these two alternatives. Jesus is reading from written scripture and is infusing that fixed tradition with new meaning.

William Temple once wrote, 'There are two duties, each relatively easy to fulfil in isolation, not easy to combine… "quench not the Spirit; hold fast to that which is good"' (*The Church Looks Forward*, p. 23). In this text Jesus announces, 'The Holy Spirit is upon me' even as he 'holds fast' to the book of Isaiah, a 'good' treasure out of the past. Paul tells the Corinthians not to go beyond scripture (1 Corinthians 4:6). At the same time in his epistle he describes great new things that God has done in Christ. Keeping that balance is not easy. May our Lord's example guide us.

2 Good news for the poor

Luke 4:16–19; Isaiah 66:1–2, 5

What is good news for the poor? Do the following lines in the text define it? If so, then 'good news for the poor' is 'release to the captives' and liberty for 'those who are oppressed'. In such a case, Jesus' ministry was to break the power of the economic, social and political chains that kept people in bondage. Or should the Greek words *euangelisasthai* (declare good news) and *keruxai* (proclaim) be followed and the text be interpreted as referring to the new reality of God, breaking into history, in Jesus Christ, to save?

Surely the key to this debate should be: What does Isaiah mean by 'the poor'? Is he primarily referring to 'those who do not have enough to eat', or does it mean 'those who sense their spiritual hunger and seek God'? Fortunately, Isaiah provides a clear answer. He uses this word overwhelmingly to refer to the humble and pious who seek God. In 66:2 the prophet writes, 'This is the man to whom I will look, he that is poor and contrite in spirit, and trembles at my word'. This same meaning for 'the poor' resurfaces in the Qumran community which used it as a means of self-designation; a community that saw itself with the right to claim the promises of God for 'the poor'.

The early Jewish Christian Church also called itself 'the poor'. Jesus says, 'Blessed are the poor in spirit' (Matthew 5:3). It is possible to read this text as an expanded version of the shorter text in Luke 6:20, 'Blessed are you poor' rather than a contradiction of it. Post-Christian Jewish texts confirm 'the poor' as meaning the pious who seek God. Indeed, 600 years of use confirm this word as meaning primarily, 'Those who tremble at the word of God' (Isaiah 66:5). To turn this word in this text into nothing more than politics and economics is to ignore history both before and after the time of Jesus. In Jesus, God 'has visited and redeemed his people'. And in each age the world needs to hear that Jesus offers hope, light and direction to those who earnestly seek communion with God. Truly this is 'good news' for all the world.

3 Release for the captives

Luke 4:16–19; Isaiah 58:6–9

Yesterday we traced the words 'the poor' and found them to mean 'the humble and pious who seek God'. Today we will look briefly at the phrase 'to proclaim release to the captives'. In our previous discussion the key proved to be, 'What did Isaiah mean?' The same key should be tried today. Isaiah 40—66 is most likely written by an inspired prophet of God who spoke to the people when they were in exile in Babylon.

Having worked for decades with Armenians and Palestinians, I know something of the special longing and pain of those who have been driven by violence from their homelands. When such peoples hear the phrase 'release to the captives' they instinctively understand it to mean 'freedom to return home'. Surely this is what Isaiah meant. To limit the word 'captivity' to some form of 'captivity to sin' is to fall into the same error we strenuously tried to avoid yesterday, namely to forget history. How then can we honour what Isaiah was saying to his readers?

The fourth line of the quotation from Luke 4:18 is borrowed from Isaiah 58:6 which discusses the kind of fasting that God really wants. God is not impressed with empty pious gestures. He asks:

Is not this the fast that I choose: to loose the bonds of wickedness, to undo the thongs of the yoke, to let the oppressed go free? Is it not to share your bread with the hungry, and bring the homeless poor into your house…?

Jesus borrows the phrase 'to let the oppressed go free' and adds it to his reading of Isaiah 61:1. The meaning of the borrowed phrase is clear. It refers to justice advocacy. Yesterday's phrase called for *proclamation*. Today's text demands *justice advocacy*. Each must be allowed its full weight if the message of Jesus and our responsibilities to a needy world are to be understood.

The 'rub' comes in fulfilling both of these commands. A brilliant example of this combination appears in the story of Zacchaeus. When Jesus accepts and loves Zacchaeus he is also easing the ever-present corrupt tax system and in this manner is freeing the people from much of their economic oppression. He engages both in proclamation and justice advocacy. May the Spirit of Christ guide us as we seek to follow in his path.

4 Compassion

Luke 4:16–19; Isaiah 42:1–7

Jesus engaged in proclamation and justice advocacy. But is that all? No, the third item on his list was *compassion*. The text reads, 'And recovery of sight to the blind'. Isaiah wrote (in Hebrew), 'The opening to those who are bound'. Does he mean the opening of the *prisons* or the opening of the *eyes* of the blind? Greek-speaking Jews before the time of Jesus translated it as 'the opening of the eyes of the blind'. Psalm 146:7–8 reads, 'The Lord sets the prisoners free; the Lord opens the eyes of the blind'. More importantly, the special suffering servant of God whom Isaiah describes in 42:7 is called to 'open the eyes that are blind, to bring out the prisoners from the dungeon'. It is this classical combination that appears in Luke 4:18.

Throughout his ministry, Jesus demonstrated a deep compassion for the people around him and on numerous occasions opened the eyes of the blind. His was a threefold ministry: *proclamation*, *justice advocacy* and *compassion*. Compassion is at the centre of the quotation and forms its climax.

Once again we are confronted with a package that too easily falls apart. Justice advocacy by itself is meaningful. But often the advocates themselves are very angry people who solve some problems and create others. Authentic justice advocacy flows from love, both of the oppressed and the oppressors. Proclamation by itself is meaningful. But at times the preacher speaks out of his or her own emotional needs rather than to the needs of the people. Justice advocacy alone cannot change the hard hearts that perpetrate injustice. Proclamation by itself ends up 'pie in the sky by and by'. Compassion alone cannot solve the problems that cause the hurts that need compassion. None of us can do all of these good things. But in the body of Christ we are a team supporting one another. Each has his or her special calling. The preacher knows that those marching for justice are an important part of the team. And those who show compassion, in whatever form, know that without a message that changes hearts, and without a just society, their work is incomplete.

May the three-faced lamp of proclamation, justice and compassion shine on us and through us to a needy world. Yes, 'and the greatest of these is love'.

5 The woman of Zarephath

Luke 4:24–27; 1 Kings 17:1, 8–16

In the synagogue Jesus recalled a famous story about Elijah. In the eighth century BC the prophet Elijah denounced King Ahab for his worship of Baal, announced a famine and then fled for his life, coming eventually to the home of a widow in Zarephath near Sidon. He found her preparing to bake a final loaf of bread for her only son. This was to be her final act before their surrender to the grim reaper. The prophet told her, 'Feed it to me!' What arrogance! How could he expect this desperate woman to feed him her last morsel of food while her starving son watched? But there is more.

According to her worldview, each god's power was limited to his own 'turf'. Yahweh could only help you if you lived in Israel. Sidon was Baal's country and the God of Israel was powerless in her district. Jonah thought he could escape Yahweh by embarking on a ship. Naaman, the visiting general from Damascus, took dirt from Israel with him on his homeward journey so that he could pray to Israel's God while living in Damascus. So how can this Baal-worshipper be expected to obey a prophet of Israel in the hope that Yahweh will help her?

She made the leap of faith and was rewarded with a cruse of oil that did not run out. Our question is: To what extent does the worldview of this woman become our worldview? Yes, the Lord of all the earth rules over the hearts of those who believe in him. But is he really Lord over Afghanistan and the land of the Rising Sun? This woman was able to break out of the worldview of her society and believe that Yahweh could touch her life in the land of Baal in Phoenicia.

May we have the faith to break the bounds of our limited perceptions of the divine, imposed on us by our society, and reach out to the Lord of lords and King of kings who is able to hear every cry and care for every need from our doorsteps to the ends of all the earth.

6 The man from Syria

Luke 4:24–27; 2 Kings 5:1–15

Jesus told a second story. Naaman was the commander of the Syrian army and a confidant of the king of Damascus,. He was then struck down with leprosy. Following a tip from his wife's maid he travelled to Israel, to the prophet Elisha, for a cure. As the commander of the Syrian army he was a powerful, dangerous man and could expect extraordinary courtesy in Israel. Custom demanded that Elisha prepare a huge banquet for the distinguished guest and at its conclusion deferentially intone, 'What can your humble servant do for you?' On arriving at the house of the prophet he was not invited in. Instead, Elisha sent a servant out to talk to him! Preposterous! Outrageous! What does he want? Ah, yes, leprosy. The prophet orders him, via a servant, to wash in the Jordan.

Naaman has the melted snows of Mount Hermon flowing through his home-town, providing the purest source of ever-flowing water in the entire Middle East. How can he be expected to lower himself and get dirty in one of Israel's muddy streams? Naaman starts home in a rage! His servants skilfully suggest that had he been asked to do some great thing he would have done it. So why not try the simple bath? He agrees, goes in and is healed.

Jesus, then, invokes the faith of this Gentile Syrian as a model for those who seek the benefits of the kingdom he has come to inaugurate. But for his audience such models were 'beyond the pale'. Like them we are also surrounded with models of faith that can speak to us from beyond ourselves. Some 60 per cent of the world's Christians are now in the two-thirds world. In the midst of unspeakable suffering their churches continue to grow at an amazing rate. Thoughtful church historians are already talking about the centre of Christianity moving to Africa and parts of Asia in the 21st century. There has been a greater influx of new believers in Jesus Christ in the South Sudan over the last 35 years than at any time or place in all of Christian history. What word from the Lord do they have for us? And are we ready to hear it coming from such a new place and people?

Guidelines

This last week we have looked briefly at some of the high points of the opening of the public ministry of our Lord as it is recorded in Luke 4:16–30. He was only 30 years old. In that society wisdom and age were closely linked. To have stood in his home synagogue and claimed to be the one on whom God's Spirit had uniquely descended and who was appointed to bring good news to the pious and set the oppressed free is amazing. Increasingly I am un-surprised that Jesus ended his earthly life on a cross. Rather, I wonder how he managed to keep talking as he did for three years. Many were indeed offended by him and yet others were drawn mysteriously to his words and his person. Perhaps we can enter that synagogue and sense afresh his unique majesty and power.

A theologian in the synagogue

Last week we began our study of the dramatic scene in the synagogue in Nazareth recorded in Luke 4:16–30. The text is so densely packed that another week will be necessary to complete an overview of its main points. By carefully editing the text of Isaiah and a daring selection of two Old Testament stories, Jesus touches on central topics in his ministry. It will be our task to reflect on six more of these throughout the coming week. They are amazingly contemporary and speak uniquely to Jesus' time and ours.

1 Theology of mission

Luke 4:16–30; Luke 15:1–7

In the text that Jesus edits and reads, and in the two stories he tells, there is a delicate balance between 'go out' and 'attract in'. The anointed one is 'sent to proclaim to the captives freedom', like Elijah who goes to the woman of Zarephath. The Messiah will also attract people in, even as Elisha attracted Naaman to come to Israel.

The force that 'goes out' is like swinging a stone around your head on a string. The force that 'attracts in' is like iron filings that are attracted to a magnet. These two forces describe two aspects of a healthy theology of mission. The first is the call that energizes us to reach out beyond ourselves in proclamation, justice advocacy and compassion. The good Samaritan ably demonstrates this theology of mission. The 'attracting in' theology is seen in the ministry of Jesus when he passes Peter and John and says, 'Follow me.' This force comes to its ultimate expression when Jesus says, 'I, when I am lifted up from the earth will draw all people to myself' (John 12:32).

These two forces of mission can be traced across church history: the force that goes out to a needy world and the force that attracts outsiders to join the fellowship of faith. The Good Shepherd needs to go out to find the lost sheep. But there also needs to be a caring community back in the village ready to help both the shepherd and the sheep on arrival. It is not easy to keep a balance between these two tasks. Sometimes we are more ready to send missionaries to other racial groups than we are to welcome those same peoples into our churches. This becomes: 'going out' is fine as long as 'coming in' is forgotten. The extreme on the other side is the voice that says, 'Whenever we celebrate the Eucharist we are *proclaiming* the Lord's death until he come. Our doors are open. This fulfils our responsibility in mission.'

Such an attitude does indeed affirm 'come in' but it ignores 'go out'. Jesus affirms both and they are parallel. If we would be loyal to what he proclaims in this text we must commit ourselves to both forces of mission and strive mightily to keep them in balance. The 'sent' and 'sending' of Elijah and Elisha must be remembered and followed.

2 The nature of faith

Luke 4: 25–30; 1 Kings 17:8–16

The great word 'faith' in the New Testament has three components: *intellectual assent*, *a daily walk of trust* and *obedience*. We need to look briefly at each of these.

Someone may say, 'I believe the bishop is telling the truth'. Here the word 'believe' has to do with intellectual assent. So with our faith. We believe God has come to us in Jesus Christ to save and many other things.

The daily walk of trust is also a critical part of faith. All of us have known people of 'great faith' who, through the deepest tragedies, have managed to maintain 'faith' in spite of unanswered questions.

Finally, faith is something we do. I *believe* I should lose ten pounds around my middle. But I usually have a 'little something' before I go to bed at night. But if I *really believed* I should lose ten pounds I would cut out the 'little something' at bedtime. Paul clarifies this understanding of faith when he writes, 'Whatsoever is not of faith is sin' (Romans 14:23, AV). We expect him to say 'Whatever is not of *faith* is *unbelief*'. But for Paul the opposite of faith is sin because when he says 'faith' he includes 'obedience'. Clearly, the opposite of obedience is sin. Thus Paul can talk about 'the obedience of faith' (Romans 1:6). For him, the two words are almost interchangeable. I *believe* I should write these meditations. I am now doing so. Thus my belief is authentic. I am acting upon it.

Both the stories in this text bring these elements together. The widow of Zarephath does not say, 'This prophet is talking nonsense. Yahweh his God cannot help me in Baal's country'. Nor does she say, 'I believe your God can help me but to give you this last loaf of bread is unthinkable'. Rather, she combines intellectual assent and obedience because she *trusts* the prophet.

In like manner, Naaman the Syrian *obeys* the command of Elisha and goes to wash in the Jordan. Intellectual assent is required. He says 'yes' with the mind and *obeys*. Without trusting the prophet, he would not have done so.

May our faith grow each day as we strive to keep all three of these elements of faith alive and strong.

3 Men and women

Luke 4:25–30; Luke 8:1–3

Jesus concluded his remarks in the synagogue with the story of a Phoenician woman from Zarephath and the tale of a military general from Damascus. This is a deliberate choice. If Jesus was looking for known stories of heroes of faith what was wrong with Abraham, Moses or David? Why one woman and one man?

Clearly, Jesus is inaugurating a new kind of fellowship in which men and women share together as equals. Luke catches this important emphasis again and again as he selects material for his Gospel. In the birth stories the angel appears to Mary and to Zechariah (Luke 1) and Jesus is presented both to Simeon and Anna (Luke 2). We read of a farmer who plants a mustard seed and of a woman who works yeast into her meal (Luke 13). There are the parables of the shepherd who loses his sheep and of the woman who loses her coin (Luke 15). But perhaps the most remarkable text, as regards men and women, is in Luke 8:1–3.

In this account we are told that Jesus is travelling from village to village with the Twelve. But with them are Mary Magdalene, Joanna and Susanna (with other women). Luke then tells us that these women were *financing the movement*! In the Wisdom of Ben Sirach we read, 'There is… great shame where a woman supports her man' (25:22). Such attitudes can be found in many cultures, both ancient and modern. Here in Luke's account women are providing the finance and travelling with the men day after day. But most shocking of all is that Luke records all of this in writing for the whole world to read!

Paul came from a Pharisaic background where social interaction between men and women was strictly limited. Yet again and again we are told in Acts that Greek women of high standing were attracted to Paul's message. Under his ministry Priscilla became a 'theological college lecturer' who instructed the famous Apollos (cf. Acts 18:26).

A new world of equality between men and women was born with the inauguration of the ministry of Jesus of Nazareth. How are we faring today as we strive to assert the full equality of women and men in the life and witness of the Church?

4 From where does the anger come?
Luke 4:24–30; Isaiah 50:4–9

Jesus read the text and then sat down. He knew that the special servant of God in Isaiah was destined to suffer. He also knew the congregation's mentality. If indeed he is the the Messiah, then his home town expects to receive some immediate material benefits. Furthermore Nazareth was a 'settler community' established by nationalistic rulers called the Maccabeans who committed themselves to territorial expansion. It is easy to imagine that the town of Nazareth likes Isaiah 61, especially from verse 4 onwards. They were there to 'build up the ancient ruins' and 'repair the ruined cities' (61:4). Verses 5 and 6 offer privileges. They read: 'Foreigners shall be your ploughmen and vine-dressers' and 'you shall eat the wealth of the nations'—a very pleasing prospect. Others will do the work and they will get all the money! Jesus, however, stops reading before coming to all that 'good stuff'. A grammatically legitimate way to translate their response is:

And all witnessed against him and were amazed at the words of mercy that proceeded out of his mouth; and they said, 'Is this not Joseph's son?' (meaning, 'Did not this young man grow up here? Does he not understand the way we feel? Why did he stop and leave the really important parts out of the reading?')

Yes, Jesus knows that the town's agenda is to reclaim land from Gentiles who have moved in from places like Zarephath up in Phoenicia and Damascus over in Syria. So he tells two stories. One is about a woman from Phoenicia and the second about a man from Damascus! Each makes a critical decision of faith and each is blessed for that decision. Jesus does not say, 'I want you to accept these Gentiles among whom you live.' Instead he announces: 'If you want the benefits of the messianic age which I have come to inaugurate, then you must *learn the nature of authentic faith from these foreigners* who were blessed by Elijah and Elisha.'

Upon listening to his words, the room explodes in anger! The congregation sees religion and politics as a single package. Jesus has disagreed with their political-economic goals, so they try to kill him. William Temple is insightful when he writes, 'Not all that the world hates is good Christianity; but it does hate good Christianity and always will' (*Readings in St John's Gospel*, pp. 271–2).

5 Jesus the rabbi

Luke 4:17–19; Mark 1:21–28

Christians across the centuries have generally seen Jesus as a simple carpenter. But our text reveals him as an astute theologian. How so? First, in a synagogue worship service he was invited to read and comment on the scriptures. Each synagogue had a salaried attendant (called the *huperetes*), who organized the worship and kept the scrolls. He was free to read the lessons, or he could invite a visiting scholar to read and comment on the text. That morning, rabbi Jesus was in attendance and the *huperetes* gave him the nod. This tells us that the community identified Jesus as a scholar.

Second, and amazingly, Jesus presumed to edit the text as he read. He omits the phrase 'to bind up the broken hearted'. He elevates the word 'call' into 'proclaim (a message)'. As we noted last week, he brings in half a verse from Isaiah 58:6 and adds it to the reading. At the end he omits the phrase 'the vengeance of our God'.

The rabbinical tradition allowed the reader to do such editing, particularly in the Prophets. But it is hard to imagine *any* reader exercising this right. By doing so, Jesus stands out as a member of the scholarly guild.

Third, Jesus interprets the Hebrew phrase 'the opening to those who are bound' to mean 'the opening of the eyes of the blind'. This interpretation connects Isaiah 61:1f to the Servant Song in Isaiah 42:7. As we have noted, such a connection had already been made by believers before the time of Jesus. But Jesus' endorsement of this identification marks him as a thoughtful scholar.

Finally, the selection of stories from the tradition are the work of a master of the scriptures. The settings for these accounts are Phoenicia and Syria, provinces that bordered on Galilee. The Gentiles who lived there were the kinds of people a settler community like Nazareth was designed to replace.

Behind the selection and editing of the text with its accompanying stories is a fearless, brilliant rabbinical mind. Jesus of Nazareth is the only candidate for this scholarly endeavour. Paul and John have always been admired as great theologians. What difference does it make to our daily discipleship when we allow ourselves to see Jesus as a scholar?

6 The cross and the resurrection
Luke 4:28–30; John 20:19–23

Many modern reconstructions of the 'real Jesus' leave us wondering, 'Why was he crucified?' Answers to this unavoidable question range from 'it was all a misunderstanding' to 'he got mixed up in politics'. Our text gives a different answer. Jesus rejected the narrow nationalism of his day. He presented two Gentiles, one of them a woman, as models of faith to be imitated. Claiming to be the anointed one of God, he refused to offer benefits on demand to his home community. He read from a text that promised wealth and leisure to study *Torah* while aliens did the farming, but he omitted the verses that offered these promises. He turned a text full of promises of privilege into a challenge to faith and responsibility. A text of judgment was transformed into a message of grace. His audience became very angry.

The rabbinical tradition stipulated that blasphemy was to be punished by stoning. Jesus uttered no blasphemy. But mobs are not usually observers of legal niceties. So he was taken to a hill outside the town for execution. This was also regulated. The culprit was to be thrown down a hill. If the fall did not cause instant death, the community at the top was to complete the task by hurling heavy stones over the cliff.

History is full of examples of one ethnic community displacing another. To accomplish such a goal the aggressors usually feel the need to demean those they are brutalizing. Words such as 'savages', 'vermin', and 'terrorists' have echoed down the centuries. When a land-grabbing venture is in progress, woe to the brave soul who dares present the victims as models of faith, especially when the aggressors are certain that God is on their side. Clearly, from this day forward Jesus knows that his message and person will continue to trigger deep and violent hostility. And what is the final result?

At the edge of the cliff, Jesus walks away! With nothing but his gentle presence, John Wesley was able to melt murderous opposition to his preaching. For our purposes, we note that Jesus comes, proclaims his message, triggers interest and then hostility. That hostility turns violent and they try to kill him—but *don't quite manage*! The thoughtful reader now has hints of how it will all end. Sunday comes after Friday in history—yes, and Sunday morning can come also in our own deeply troubled lives and societies.

Guidelines

As we noted, it is not easy for a young man to get a serious hearing in his home town. The Middle East has always respected age, and a young man in his early thirties is expected to listen and learn when in the presence of his elders.

Thus we fully expect Jesus to attempt to please. Surely he will let his elders know that he is a 'good boy' who supports the traditional values of the community. He will encourage their efforts to reclaim the countryside from the aliens and emphasize the importance of sabbath laws. Some comments on the tithe and a word or two about food laws will be in place. He can add some guarded comments on the Roman occupation and how the Messiah will bring relief from injustice.

But no! No attempt to limit himself to their agenda is made. Boldly and uncompromisingly Jesus announces his agenda of proclamation, justice advocacy and compassion to be carried out by himself as the anointed one of God. They can join him by imitating the remarkable faith of this Phoenician woman and of Naaman the Syrian. He knows his editing of the text of Isaiah 61 will cause anger. It is a risk he was willing to take. May we contemplate afresh who he was and what he came to inaugurate in our lives and in our world.

THE SABBATH

Recently someone explained to me some Latin: how the word for 'business'—*negotium*—is the negative of the word for 'leisure'—*otium*. The moment God created humankind, according to Genesis 1 and 2, he stopped for some *otium*. The Latin terms express well the priority: how leisure is integral to the state of blessing for which we were created. Work is merely its negative, its absence.

This is the essence of the Sabbath rule, given by God for our flourishing. Its appropriation has a rather speckled history: the Israelites may have overplayed it, Jesus challenged it, Paul virtually dismissed it. Yet the creation principle, whereby God created the world in six days and rested on the seventh, is still maintained as a point of reference in much of the biblical literature. This season of holidays is a time of holy-days, for discovering afresh God's priorities and God's gift of rest, of blessing, of wholeness and holiness.

---

1 The crown of creation

Genesis 1:1—2:4a

The first account of creation presents us with a neat and tidy picture of the ordered way in which God proceeds to create the heavens and the earth, from nothingness to completion. For each of six days he performs a particular work of creation—and before nightfall each day he declares each as 'good'. And on the seventh day, God 'rested... from all the work that he had done' (2:2). Here is the principle from which, it is claimed, the Sabbath command is derived (see, for example, Exodus 20:8–11).

Imagine reading this account for the first time. What would you expect to happen on day seven? The account gathers momentum, as if to stress that there is something even more sophisticated, even more important, than the creation of humankind on the sixth day. Indeed there is, although it is a rather different kind of activity and it comes as a surprise. Rather than the work of creation, there is the cessation of work, the 'activity' of rest. This is the climax of the story, the focus of all God's work—the establishment of the seventh day, and its hallowing as a day of rest. Does this suggest that rest is more important than work? Certainly on the seventh day it is. Indeed, it appears to be the goal of the preceding six days of work. Moreover, it is the first day for humankind.

The position of this text at the beginning of the Bible, whatever its literary origins, suggests that there is some priority given here for all that follows. The whole story is about blessing, and the Sabbath is a celebration at its culmination. Just as God looks at the end of each day during his work of creation and declares it 'good', so God spends a day at the end of six days of work resting and enjoying the fruits of his work. If we are to follow God's lead and rest on the Sabbath, then we are to understand it as a holy day meant for 'holiday', for satisfaction and for joy, for well-being and blessing. It is not a day to dread, as a friend of mine described his strict and solemn childhood experience when he was not allowed to play games or watch TV on Sunday. When keeping Sabbath is a burden, then it is counter-productive and something is wrong.

2 Becoming holy

Exodus 31:12–17

In another priestly statement about Sabbath, it is affirmed that keeping Sabbath is a way to know God and his commitment to his world: 'You shall keep my sabbaths… in order that you may know that I, the Lord, sanctify you' (v. 13).

To know God is to love God, and to love God is to do his will. What is it that we may know better about God by keeping his Sabbath? It is that we may understand better the character of the Lord—Yahweh—as the one who sanctifies, the one who is holy and delights in making others holy. God's people, made in his image, are called upon to imitate him and become like him in his holiness. This is made especially clear at Mount Sinai when God forms a covenant with Israel (Exodus 19:4–6). It is confirmed throughout the Pentateuch: consider, for example, the refrain through Leviticus, 'Be holy as I am holy.'

The Sabbath command takes us back to God's activity at creation, reminding us of God's power and simultaneously his delight. God's will is that we enjoy the creation and find blessing in it, and keeping the Sabbath faithfully week by week is an announcement of trust in this God of power and delight. Resting on the Sabbath is an assertion that life does not depend on any feverish activity. God is in charge and his work is complete. We may pause from work because God paused from work—and remember that everything in life, even that which we may work for, comes to us ultimately because it is *given* to us. It challenges the so-called 'Protestant work ethic' that underpins so much contemporary Western culture.

God's holiness is something he gives to us, yet it does not drop from heaven. We grow in holiness when we strive to be like God. At creation he gave an example; at Mount Sinai, in making the covenant, he invited Israel to follow it; and here, in the law—given because Israel accepted the invitation—he instructs them to obey it. Although the language has changed from what God gives and what he does in Genesis 2 to '*You shall* keep the Sabbath' (vv. 13, 14, 16), the grace is still evident. The law is given to help Israel imitate God and maintain their side of the covenant. If the tone is stern, it is because the consequences of disobeying (having just promised enthusiastically to obey) are tragic.

3 Holiness and justice

Deuteronomy 5:1–21

A Sabbath command that is purely a prohibition from work could, of course, become a licence for laziness, which is far from imitating and trusting God. Although some biblical scholars suggest that the command is confined to the Priestly writer(s), and some Protestants have sometimes dismissed the prohibition as 'mere' Old Testament legalism, there is much more to the reality and scope of the gift. We miss out if we explain it away.

In Deuteronomy's record of the Sinai commandment, keeping the Sabbath day holy also involves protecting children and slaves and animals and foreigners. Here is an example of the law being read and taught (cf. 2 Chronicles 17:9): in this exposition the Sabbath is developed to involve principles of justice in Israelite society. The Israelites are to show concern for the powerless because they too were powerless and oppressed. As God delivered Israel from Egypt, so Israel is to deliver those who live on the margins within their own society. The same principle applies: *imitatio dei*, the imitation of God.

A few years ago in Britain there was a 'Keep Sunday Special' campaign prior to a parliamentary decision concerning Sunday trading. It was commonly felt that the campaign failed, given that legislation now allows for supermarkets and other retail outlets to open on Sundays. However, in at least one respect this campaign was very effective. One of the grounds on which the campaign was conducted was for the protection of those who worked in the retail sector. As a result it is, thankfully, rare for employees to be *obliged* to work on Sundays. The provision of a Sabbath is not to be a luxury for the wealthy or powerful, but an opportunity for all people to acknowledge God's grace and blessing.

The Sabbath rest of God is an invitation to join a new kind of human community—one which believes that God has given it everything it needs for living fully, and thus one which has the resources for caring for all members of society, no matter what their background or circumstances. During the exile, when Israel's normal forms of worship were banished, the keeping of Sabbath became the external badge of identity for this new community. It also served as the means for sustaining the community. As the Jewish writer Ahad Ha'am stated, 'More than the Jews kept Shabbat, Shabbat kept the Jews.'

4 Lord of the Sabbath

Matthew 12:1–14

There is a great debate in the Gospels on the subject of Sabbath observance. The two Sabbath controversies of Matthew 12 (with parallels in Mark 2—3 and Luke 6 and 14) illustrate how its purpose had become distorted, such that it had turned into a day of petty restrictions and burdensome legislation. Strangely and tragically, those who are most anxious to *protect* the Bible's message can *destroy* that message by a false zeal for scripture. So now they accuse the one who had said, 'Whoever breaks one of the least of these commands... will be called least in the kingdom of heaven' (Matthew 5:19) of doing 'what is not right' or 'not biblical' (v. 2). Jesus seems to ignore the fact that scripture at its highest place—in the Ten Commandments—says clearly that on the Sabbath day 'you shall not do any work' (Exodus 20:10).

Jesus challenges the Pharisees for keeping the commandment in the wrong way for the wrong reasons. In quick succession he pulls a Davidic example out of the historical books (1 Samuel 21:1–6), a priestly example out of the law (Numbers 28:9–10), and a saying from the prophets (Hosea 6:6), to show the people of God that they have more freedom under scripture than their teachers gave them. His quotation from Hosea affirms the point of the law—for wide-hearted sympathy, not scrupulous self-sacrifice. The Pharisees had 'lost the plot'. The Sabbath is not a matter for Jewish national pride. Rather, it is God's gift at creation: thus Israel neither owns it nor controls it. Furthermore, Jesus has taken the place of both law and temple: he is Lord, Lord of the Sabbath (v. 8).

The second situation (vv. 9–14) underlines how the Sabbath is designed to enrich life, as a reminder of God's gifts, not as something to burden life. Jesus explains how the healing of the man with a withered hand makes sense. The Sabbath command was intended for human welfare—a 'holiday' for workers, a command devoted to community renewal—not for religious showing off. The saving God does not want to be placed on hold for 24 hours while people hurt. He wants humankind (indeed, animals too) to be refreshed from their work, to rest, to find peace and to be made whole.

5 O Sabbath rest

John 19:31—20:23

The Sabbath controversies have left Christians confused as to how to observe the Sabbath in gospel times. On the one hand Jesus upholds the law, and on the other hand he challenges it. At the same time Jesus fulfils it.

Because humanity is made in the image of God, God's rest described in Genesis 2 is a promised rest for humanity. It is this promise that Jesus fulfils with the invitation, 'Come to me, all you that are weary and are carrying heavy burdens, and I will give you rest...' (Matthew 11:28–30). Whereas Israel in exile had emphasized the role of keeping Sabbath for effecting restoration (consider the stress given to the prohibition concerning heavy burdens on the Sabbath in Jeremiah 17:21ff.), Jesus is here declaring the end of exile. We are invited to find God's Sabbath rest, ultimately, through Christ. Jesus takes a day of rest himself when his work is complete. Hans Urs von Balthasar, in his book on Holy Saturday, suggests that God's Sabbath rest after creation somehow foreshadows Jesus' rest in the tomb on Holy Saturday.

Christian tradition has moved Sabbath observance from Saturday to Sunday. It was 'early on the first day of the week...' (John 20:1) that God wrought his new work of creation. Thus the *ecclesia*, the gathering of God's people for worship, takes place most appropriately on this first day of the week, the day of resurrection.

Aside from this gathering as the Church, the practices of desisting from work and marking the Sabbath as holy are varied. This unity and diversity are, I suggest, quite appropriate. That which constitutes rest and provides refreshment from work will differ with each individual's interests and occupation. At the same time, the ultimate form of rest is discovered through worship.

6 The enduring promise of rest

Hebrews 4:1–11

There is some future expectation with regard to the Sabbath. Colossians 2:16–17 is suggestive: 'Do not let anyone condemn you in matters of... sabbaths. These are only a shadow of what is to come.' Whatever this means, it affirms some further future fulfilment, and this is corroborated in the letter to the Hebrews.

Hebrews 4:9 states, 'A sabbath rest still remains for the people of God.' Through the joining of quotations from Genesis 2:2 and Psalm 95:11, the author of Hebrews affirms in verses 3–11 that the promised 'sabbath rest' still anticipates a complete realization for the people of God in the eschatological end-time that had been inaugurated with the appearance of Jesus (Hebrews 1:1–3).

This 'sabbath rest' is not some future Sabbath celebration in heaven that follows the second coming. Nor is it the rest that comes in death. The text points to a present reality of rest in which those 'who have believed are entering' (v. 3) that is connected with a future reality of rest (v. 11). The physical 'sabbath rest' (*sabbatismos*) of ceasing from 'works' (v. 10) in commemoration of God's rest at creation (v. 4; cf. Genesis 2:2) is the weekly outward manifestation of the inner experience of spiritual rest (*katapausis*) in which the final eschatological rest is already experienced 'today' (v. 7). Thus the Sabbath habit combines in itself past, present and future. It involves the commemoration of creation, the experience of salvation and the anticipation of the end times.

Notice the theological shape of this reflection. In regard to the Sabbath, this passage reminds us of the basic shape of Christian theology as a whole. The basic shape of all biblical theology is creation, covenant and eschatology: one God who made the world; one God who yearns to renew the world, and, in the middle, the covenant as the means by which the creator God is renewing the face of his world. This is, of course, the shape of the creed. So for Christians, believers in the new covenant, the gift of the Sabbath is a gift for remembering God's faithfulness in the past, living out Christ's salvation in the present, and looking forward to the future. This is *rest* as it was, is and ever shall be. Amen!

Guidelines

O Sabbath rest by Galilee! O calm of hills above,
where Jesus knelt to share with Thee
the silence of eternity, interpreted by love.

Drop Thy still dews of quietness, till all our strivings cease;
take from our souls the strain and stress,
and let our ordered lives confess the beauty of Thy peace.

JOHN G. WHITTIER (1807–92)

ALSO PUBLISHED BY BRF

NEW DAYLIGHT

New Daylight offers a devotional approach to reading and understanding the Bible. Each issue covers four months of daily Bible readings and reflection from a regular team of contributors, who represented a stimulating mix of church backgrounds, from Baptist to Anglican Franciscan! Each day's reading provides a Bible passage (text included), comment and prayer or thought for reflection. In *New Daylight* the Sundays and special festivals from the Church calendar are noted on the relevant days, to help you grow more familiar with the rhythm of the Christian year.

DAY BY DAY WITH GOD

Day by Day with God (published jointly with Christina Press) is written especially by women for women, with a regular team of contributors. Each four-monthly issue offers daily Bible readings, with key verses printed out, helpful comment and a prayer for the day ahead.

HOW TO ORDER BRF NOTES

If you have enjoyed reading this sampler and would like to order the dated notes on a regular basis, they can be obtained through:

CHRISTIAN BOOKSHOPS

Most Christian bookshops stock BRF notes and books. You can place a regular order with your bookshop for yourself or for your church. For details of your nearest stockist please contact the BRF office.

INDIVIDUAL SUBSCRIPTION

For yourself

By placing an annual subscription for BRF notes, you can ensure you will receive your copy regularly. We also send you additional information about BRF: BRF News, information about our new publications and updates about our ministry activities.

You can also order a subscription for three years (two years for *Day by Day with God*), for an even easier and more economical way to obtain your Bible reading notes.

Gift subscription

Why not give a gift subscription to *New Daylight*, *Guidelines* or *Day by Day with God* to a friend or family member? Simply complete all parts of the order form on the next page and return it to us with your payment. You can even enclose a message for the gift recipient.

For either of the above, please complete the 'Individual Subscription Order Form' and send with your payment to BRF.

CHURCH SUBSCRIPTION

If you order, directly from BRF, five or more copies from our Bible reading notes range of *New Daylight*, *Guidelines* or *Day by Day with God*, they will be sent post-free. This is known as a church subscription and it is a convenient way of bulk-ordering notes for your church. There is no need to send payment with your initial order. Please complete the 'Church Subscriptions Order Form' and we will send you an invoice with your first delivery of notes.

- **Annual subscription:** you can place a subscription for a full year, receiving one invoice for the year. Once you place an annual church subscription, you will be sent the requested number of Bible reading notes automatically. You will also receive useful information to help you run your church group. You can amend your order at any time, as your requirements increase or decrease. Church subscriptions run from May to April of each year. If you start in the middle of a subscription year, you will receive an invoice for the remaining issues of the current subscription year.

- **Standing order:** we can set up a standing order for your Bible reading notes order. Approximately six to seven weeks before a new edition of the notes is due to start, we will process your order and send it with an invoice.

CHURCH SUBSCRIPTIONS

Name _____

Address _____

_____

_____ Postcode _____

Telephone Number_____

E-mail _____

Church _____

Denomination _____

Name of Minister _____

Please start my order from Jan/May/Sep* *(delete as applicable)*

I would like to pay annually/receive an invoice each issue of the notes
(delete as applicable)

Please send me:	**Quantity**
New Daylight	_____
New Daylight Large Print	_____
Guidelines	_____
Day by Day with God	_____

Please do not enclose payment. We have a fixed subscription year for Church Subscriptions, which is from May to April each year. If you start a Church Subscription in the middle of a subscription year, we will invoice you for the number of issues remaining in that year.

GLSAM03

BRF is a Registered Charity

INDIVIDUAL & GIFT SUBSCRIPTIONS

☐ I would like to give a gift subscription (please complete both name and address sections below)
☐ I would like to take out a subscription myself (complete name and address details only once)

This completed coupon should be sent with appropriate payment to BRF. Alternatively, please write to us quoting your name, address, the subscription you would like for either yourself or a friend (with their name and address), the start date and credit card number, expiry date and signature if paying by credit card.

Gift subscription name _____

Gift subscription address _____

_____ Postcode _____

Please send beginning with the May / September / January issue: *(delete as applicable)*

(please tick box)	**UK**	**SURFACE**	**AIR MAIL**
New Daylight	☐ £11.10	☐ £12.45	☐ £14.70
New Daylight 3-year sub	☐ £27.45		
New Daylight LARGE PRINT	☐ £16.80	☐ £20.40	☐ £24.90
Guidelines	☐ £11.10	☐ £12.45	☐ £14.70
Guidelines 3-year sub	☐ £27.45		
Day by Day with God	☐ £12.15	☐ £13.50	☐ £15.75
Day by Day with God 2-year sub	☐ £20.40		

Please complete the payment details below and send your coupon, with appropriate payment to: BRF, First Floor, Elsfield Hall, 15–17 Elsfield Way, Oxford OX2 8FG.

Your name _____

Your address _____

_____ Postcode _____

Total enclosed £ _____ (cheques should be made payable to 'BRF')

Payment by ☐ cheque ☐ postal order ☐ Visa ☐ Mastercard ☐ Switch

Card number: ☐☐☐☐ ☐☐☐☐ ☐☐☐☐ ☐☐☐☐ ☐☐☐☐

Expiry date of card: ☐☐ ☐☐   Issue number (Switch): ☐☐☐

Signature _____ Date / /
(essential if paying by credit/Switch card)
GLSAM03   *BRF is a Registered Charity*

BIBLE READING NOTES

Available from your local Christian bookshop

First Floor, Elsfield Hall, 15–17 Elsfield Way,
Oxford OX2 8FG, England
Tel: 01865 319700; Fax: 01865 319701
E-mail: enquiries@brf.org.uk; Website: www.brf.org.uk

For your nearest stockist, please contact brf

---

www.brf.org.uk

brf — Resourcing your spiritual journey

Enter an author, title, subject or phrase   Books ○ Extracts/Info ●   **go**

- Home
- Bible Centre
- Book news
- Events
- Articles
- Authors
- Who is BRF?

Welcome to BRF

For Bible based resources and information for today's Christian living and for details of all BRF publications, extracts and articles, and a wealth of other information.

Find out about:

- New BRF publications

- BRF's comprehensive range of resources:
  Bible reading and study; Prayer and spirituality; Lent and Advent

- BRF authors

- Quiet days, Retreats and other events

- Barnabas (storybooks, seasonal activity books and teaching resources for 3–11 year olds)

- The Barnabas Live Creative Arts and Schools Programme

The Bible Reading Fellowship
First Floor
Elsfield Hall
15–17 Elsfield Way
Oxford
OX2 8FG
England
Tel 01865 319700
Fax 01865 319701
E-mail
enquiries@brf.org.uk

Visit the BRF website at www.brf.org.uk

BRF is a Registered Charity

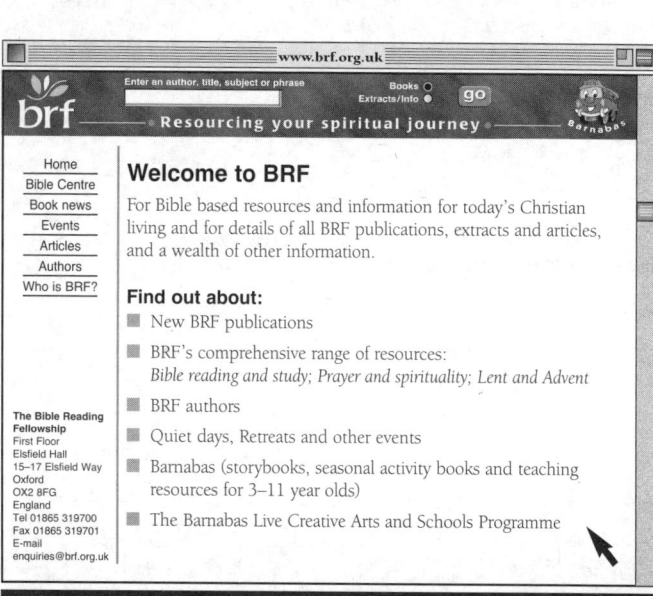